Unlocking the Power of
Single Parenting

Lucie Muchina

Unlocking the Power of Single Parenting

Copyright © 2021 Lucie Muchina

All rights reserved. No part of this publication may be reproduced, stored in a retrieval system, or transmitted, in any form or by any means, electronic, mechanical, photocopying, recording or otherwise without the prior permission of Lucie Muchina.

All Scripture quotations, unless otherwise indicated, are taken from the Holy Bible, New International Version, UK edition, copyright © 1973, 1978, 1984 by International Bible Society. Published by Hodder and Stoughton. Used by permission. All rights reserved.

Scripture quotations marked NLT are taken from the Holy Bible, New Living Translation, copyright © 1996, 2004, 2007 by Tyndale House Foundation. Used by permission of Tyndale House Publishers, Inc., Carol Stream, Illinois 60188. All rights reserved.
www.newlivingtranslation.com | www.tyndale.com

Scripture quotations marked NKJV are taken from the New King James Version. Copyright © 1982 by Thomas Nelson, Inc. Used by permission. All rights reserved.

ISBN: 978-0-9928315-2-3

Acknowledgements

Voltaire, a French Enlightenment writer and historian, described appreciation as a wonderful thing: 'one that makes what is excellent in others belong to us as well'.

I would first of all like to thank God for making this book a reality and enabling me to share my story. It took a lot to be able to share my personal experiences but, as I found out, this contributed to the healing process.

Secondly, I would like to express profound gratitude to my pastor, Osien Sibanda, for his support and insight and the contributions he made to the material in this book. I'm also immensely grateful to Geoff Watson, a colleague who I've worked with for years and who kindly helped with the editing and contributed to the content of this book. Special thanks, Geoff - may the Lord reward you for your kindness. To my friend, Faith Khisa, thank you for standing with me in difficult times, including when I was too stubborn to refuse help from anyone.

Finally, I want to express my sincere appreciation to my sons, Alvin and Jeff. You are a special blessing to me. To my husband, and the father of our sons, Duncan, who at the time of concluding this book was now part of the family - thank you for giving me a reason to write this book and be a voice for single parents.

This is a book based on real life events. Whenever situations or names are quoted, names have been altered to preserve anonymity.

Contents

INTRODUCTION 7

CHAPTER 1
The background to single parenting 11

CHAPTER 2
Personal experiences 17

CHAPTER 3
Friends' stories 23

CHAPTER 4
Biblical examples of single mothers 29

CHAPTER 5
The impact of single parenting on the parent 35

CHAPTER 6
The impact of single parenting on children 39

CHAPTER 7
Single parenting and society 45

CHAPTER 8:
Things I've learnt as a single parent 47

CHAPTER 9
Final thoughts 53

REFERENCES 57

BOOKS BY LUCIE MUCHINA 58

Introduction

YOU HAVE PROBABLY heard the good old saying that parenting is one of the most fulfilling roles in life. That's true - but it's also the one role where you qualify before undertaking any training or completing a test! It should come as no surprise that the journey of parenting is a mixture of bumps, happiness and sometimes accidents along the way.

For most people, parenting is an exciting, satisfying yet uncertain journey. It's one where mothers, fathers and carers learn something new at every stage of their child's life. This learning never ceases because 'once a parent, always a parent', even when the children have grown up into adults.

Whilst satisfying in itself, parenting was never meant for one person alone. Most parents have reported that the parenting journey is one fraught with a wide range of emotions stemming from frustration to great fulfilment, all happening at the same time. However, it's fair to say that this rollercoaster of emotions is much more intense for those doing it single-handedly.

In His creation, God said that 'it is not good for man to be alone' and that 'two are better than one' (Gen 2:18). These Bible passages explain the power of having support mechanisms in a family, so that, if either person were to fall down, the other person would help them up. The Scriptures used in this context are based on marriage but are very much relevant to the role of parenting. The expression 'It takes two to tango' couldn't be more true.

The Bible explains that man and woman were created to live together in order to bring up 'godly offspring' (Malachi 2:15). The concept of 'godly offspring' has been challenged over the years by situations and circumstances in individual or family lives, resulting sometimes in single-led households. A good example is the story of Hagar (found in the book of Genesis) who had to bring up her son Ishmael as a single parent (see Chapter 5 of this book for more details).

We live in a world where people are free to make independent choices. Some people have chosen to live single lives and raise children single-handedly. In other cases, people find themselves in situations that are out of their control. Whatever the situation, the impact on the parent and the children is significant and worth exploring.

The challenges faced by single households cannot in general terms be compared with those where both parents are present and cannot be ignored any longer. As a society, understanding how to support single households will go a long way to improve their lives, including those of their children and future generations. The 'choice' of single parenting is not for everyone and, for the majority of single parents, this is not a 'choice' at all. I have talked to a significant number of single parents who have shared their difficult experiences, and I describe some of their stories in Chapter 3.

Introduction

I have lived as a single parent for many years. In this book, I share my experiences and discuss the impact of single parenting on the parents and children, and also the opportunities society has to support single parents in difficult situations. I identify Biblical and other examples of single parents and how they overcame these challenges. In addition, I provide examples of real-life experiences of women with dependent children who have faced difficult challenges.

I hope this book will help you to understand not just the challenges of single parenting but the untapped power of single parents in successfully bringing up children. In addition to examples of single parenthood, there are tips on how single parents can take care of themselves in order to live a deeply fulfilled life.

The Background to Single Parenting

Chapter 1

IN TODAY'S WORLD, it's a mammoth task to be a parent, even when both parents are present. This is due to many different demands (especially when children are young) and can include financial burdens, childcare resources and having to juggle work and school runs etc. For the single parent, this is even harder, and worse still for those on a low income. The inability to afford childcare, take a sick day off, and only take rest when the child falls asleep can take a toll on anyone's life. There is the added disadvantage of having no one to share the enchanting moments and tantrums with and no one to reassure you that you are doing just fine.

Statistics from across the globe paint a grim picture of this issue. Information obtained from the Office of National Statistics (ONS) indicate that, in the United Kingdom in 2017, there were 1.6 million lone mothers with dependent children. The report goes on to explain that the weekly cost of a lone parent's first child is more expensive when compared to a child that is raised by two parents. This can perhaps be attributed to the added cost of childcare to allow the parent to work.

The report goes on to explain that this trend continues throughout the first seventeen years of the child's life and that the most expensive period regarding the weekly cost of a dependent child's life in a lone-parent household occurs within the first two years, before decreasing thereafter, until the age of eleven. The financial implications for the single parent are real, including added demands to juggle between work and childcare.

The trend is similar in the United States where, according to the Single Mother Guide, an educational site in the United States for single parents, about 4 out 10 children were born to unwed mothers in 2017. Nearly two-thirds were born to mothers under the age of 30 years. Research estimates that 1 in 4 children under the age of 18 - a total of about 17.2 million - are currently being raised without a father. Of all the single-parent families in the U.S., single mothers make up by far the majority.

The Church itself has not been spared this epidemic and has seen high profile relationships ending in divorce within its own numbers. At the time of writing this book, an internationally renowned church leader has recently left his wife of many years with five children in her care. The wife suddenly found herself being a single parent overnight with devastated children. The impact on the family and the church as a whole was unbearable. At about the same time, another famous television personality also left his wife of several years, with children hit hard by the circumstances.

The statistics, which make for sad reading, illustrate the serious nature of this epidemic and its impact on those most vulnerable in our society. The single parent is often left exhausted and disappointed and, unless supported, it takes a long time for them to rise again. However, the church and the community at large can positively engage with single parents and, by extension, the children growing up in these households, and make a very positive impact on their lives.

What is 'Single Parenting'?

Collins dictionary defines a single parent as one who is bringing up a child on their own because the other parent is not living with them. There are various reasons why people find themselves living as single parents. This might include divorce, widowhood, widower, women who choose to have a baby without a partner or separation.

Historically, the death of a spouse was a common cause of single parenting. Often, this was brought about by disease or wars. However, with improvements in healthcare, especially in industrialised countries, the mortality rates of those of reproductive age has significantly reduced over the past century, making death a far less common cause of single parenting.

Rates of divorce and separation, on the other hand, have risen exponentially in recent times. Whilst every relationship is different and complex to understand, the relative ease of divorce in the West in the 21st century could be a contributory factor. In today's world, it only takes less than a day to formalise a divorce whilst, in previous times, this would take months if not years.

In other parts of the world, a couple would have to go through a complex, traditional process before they could be legally divorced. This lengthy process - clearly put in place to discourage divorce - could be exhausting even for those determined to end their marriage. Selwyn Hughes, in his book Marriage as God Intended, notes that the statistics concerning the state of marriage in the 21st century make for depressing reading. He goes on to argue that societal views of marriage have changed dramatically over the years. Recent divorce statistics from the Office of National Statistics indicate that 42% of marriages in England and Wales end in divorce.

Separation occurs when spouses in a marriage stop living together without getting divorced. Married couples may separate as an initial step in the divorce process or to gain a perspective on the marriage to determine if a divorce is what they want.

Researchers have found that the average separation lasts a year or less. For couples who are eventually reconciled, most do so within the first two years. Beyond two years, there is little chance that a couple will be reconciled. Many couples who end up divorcing do so after three or four years of separation.

The trend of births to unmarried women has changed over the years. Women are now often leaving it until later in order to have a baby, either with or without a partner. A significant number are doing so in order to climb the career ladder or, for others, in order to pursue an independent life.

For many modern couples, marriage is not something they wish to consider, for a variety of reasons, and many are content to have children within a long-term relationship or within a civil partnership. Statistics suggest that these types of relationship are just as likely to fail as traditional marriages, so can also lead to single parenthood.

Every single parent's journey is different and, whilst there are more single mothers than single fathers, the experiences are very different for each one of them and never easy.

Why does 'Single Parenting' exist?

Most people believe that a healthy marriage is the best recipe to bring stability for the couple as well as the children in the family. Couples can share with each other life's joys and challenges. Some argue that marriage is the single most effective antidote to family breakdown. There are of course other benefits, including financial stability, companionship and joint support for children.

No couples go into marriage having sworn: 'Till we separate or divorce'!. There is always an acknowledgement of commitment and love at the start of a marriage. What happens down the line, when things go wrong, is a question that cannot be addressed by a single answer. In those situations it is all too easy to question a myriad of issues, for example whether the two individuals went through any preparation before they entered into marriage, or whether both parties were fully committed to each other in the first place. Whatever the situation, every relationship is different and this has to be looked at in its own right.

The following quote from an article in the Independent newspaper (2018) on failed relationships, was thought provoking:

'The commitment required to get married works in keeping couples together during the rough times that occur in any relationship'. This statement clearly illustrates the hard work required to keep a couple together.

Personal Experiences   Chapter 2

THE WORLD OF a single parent is a bit of a quagmire in many ways. It is a life that is not clearly understood, even by those who find themselves living in it, unless they've planned it - which is the minority. For some, the reasons for becoming a single parent is an area that is best left alone as it provokes painful memories, and for others the topic ignites lots of questions with no concrete answers.

A friend of mine (although happily married) recently attended a workshop that had been organised for single mothers. She wanted to understand how she could support a special friend who was a single parent. As part of the workshop, single mothers freely shared their lived experiences in an honest way in what was a safe space. This was a good way for the women to provide moral support for each other and was clearly having a positive impact. My friend, a mother of two, found the workshop very inspiring but she was not prepared for what she heard in the discussions.

She told me that the experiences shared by the single mothers who attended caused her great distress. She was candid enough to say that she never knew people lived in such difficulty while showing little of this impact on the outside. I have to add that my friend has always had her husband by her side and this experience was one that she couldn't resonate with and had clearly left her speechless. My friend's experience is not an isolated one: those close to single parents, as well as wider society, struggle to comprehend the life of a single parent.

Whilst the notion of single parenting is not new and has existed since the beginning of humanity, society still struggles to understand the magnitude of the challenges faced by single parents. Whether it's a life choice or not, single parents make do with what they have in very difficult circumstances. Due to the stigma attached to being a single parent, many find it difficult to talk about their situation or seek help. The need to understand the life of a single parent is therefore critical in order to effectively support them and their children, which will in turn contribute towards achieving a cohesive community.

In the following chapters, I'll be sharing some aspects of my life as a single parent. I'll also share true (anonymised) stories of single parents and some biblical examples of single parents and how they managed to wade through the storms of life.

My Story

I'm a mother of two boys and was a single parent for well over 15 years. As a young girl, I was brought up in a close-knit home in Kenya and was always close to my parents. As such, I wanted to do them proud and what better way than to 'marry right', according to the way I was brought up, adhering to church standards. My church wedding was spectacular and, with my father walking me down the aisle, there was never a prouder moment for both of us. My daddy was to hand me over to a man I had known and loved for several years and I was ready to commit to spend my life with him. It was that 'wow moment' that most young women dream of.

The preparations for the wedding had started months before the wedding day. The ladies on the wedding line-up had spent the previous day pampering me with all sorts of beauty products. The hair stylist had to sleep over to make sure the hair style was just right. The gown was flown in from abroad and arrived just in time. This was the moment I'd been waiting for all those years and I was ready to celebrate it. The wedding was attended by masses of people, invited or not(!), which made it really special.

Such was the excitement of the celebration that I forgot I was wearing my wedding gown and danced the night away.

My husband and I had a great start to our marriage and decided to emigrate to England and start a new life. This we did with no problem as I had already settled there and was working there. After a year of marriage, our first child came along and brought great joy to us, our family and friends. My husband was by this time running businesses abroad and would travel frequently. Our second child came along three years later and, again, we were all filled with excitement. My husband continued travelling abroad and would spend several months away. He would return home for just a few months and would go away again for another lengthy period. This was starting to cause strain on our marriage but he was determined to continue to travel and run his businesses.

Meanwhile, work was taking a toll on me, and having to bring up two young children on my own for most of the time was stressful. Finance was a big problem, as was childcare, work - you name it - and it was all happening before my eyes. I was unable to explain what was happening to me, partly because I was naïve and wanted to ignore what I was beginning to suspect was happening. I went into a very dark hole and had by this time lost count of the frequent business trips. On his last trip, my husband was away for a very long time.

Life simply went from bad to worse. I was running like a headless chicken between jobs, childcare and home. I would leave my children with whoever would care to have them in order to go to work. I needed bills to be paid, food on the table and the list of needs was endless. I would cry the whole night and wake up with swollen, red eyes. How I didn't go into a deep depression still remains a mystery.

My fears had come true and I was to learn eventually that my estranged husband had by this time moved in with another woman and there was no way for him to turn back. How was I to bring up my children on my own? And how about work? I needed to work and sustain the family! Was there any way of coming out of this? Was there anyone out there to listen to me? I didn't even have time to look after myself. I cannot tell you the number of times I wore clothes inside out during the dark winter season, only to realise this when the day broke. The climax to all this was when I wore different coloured shoes to work one day and only noticed at lunchtime! Thankfully this turned into laughter, and I was relieved as I had not laughed properly for years.

However, things were not getting any easier for me. I was getting very worried about my children, who would cry daily for their father. This I found the most difficult thing of all. What was I going to tell them? It was one thing for their father to leave but another for them not to understand the reasons behind his actions, with their limited understanding. I remember vividly when one of my sons wrote a letter while in school. The teacher handed this to me when I went to collect him. In the letter was a note to his father pleading for him to come home and a prayer that whatever business his father was doing would go well so he could find time to come and see him. My son had then put a picture of a large tear drop! I cannot explain how this broke my heart. Knowing how my son felt and not being able to help him was difficult to bear. I'm not sure how I managed to sleep that night. However, I learnt how to pray and spend time alone with God who became a very close friend to me. As I write, this relationship is one that's still very special to me. I needed someone to pour my heart out to and I had a close confidant. One who would not judge me, One who understood the pain and One who was also interested in the affairs of my children.

In addition, the lonely nights started getting less lonely as I started to focus on keeping myself busy with various projects. I completed my Masters course during this time, recorded two music albums and wrote a book. Incredible! But just what I needed at this time. Something to take my attention from the pain I was going through and focus the energy on something more productive.

Meanwhile, my children continued to grow, albeit supported by friends and family, all of whom I'll forever be grateful to. My father would call me up and encourage me. He would tell me that things would be fine. In addition, a close friend decided to stick with me during this time. I was her 'assignment'; and she held on to me, prayed for me and kept in touch on a weekly basis. She's on my list of special people I will be forever grateful to.

At the time of writing, things have become much better and, whilst time is not a complete healer, it's a reflection of where I've come from and how far God has brought me.

Friends' Stories Chapter 3

Karen's Story

My friend Karen was a single mother of three children, two boys and one girl, all aged under 10 years of age. She worked at a local supermarket as a Marketing Executive. Karen had been a single mother since the birth of her youngest daughter. Her husband Joe (the father of all three children) had left the home when the youngest child was born.

Karen and Joe were childhood sweethearts and grew up in the same neighbourhood. Their memories of love dated back as far as their pre-school years. They attended the same primary school and they continued seeing each other in secondary school, and this went on into their university years. Their relationship was well known to their friends who described them as the perfect couple. Upon finishing his university education, Joe did not waste time in proposing to his childhood sweetheart, who was over the moon. The spectacular engagement event was graced by family and friends who came in large numbers to witness what everyone had been looking forward to. A year later, the couple started making plans for their wedding. This was a much greater celebration, with hundreds of friends attending to witness the joining together of the two lovebirds in holy matrimony.

Karen looked stunning and so did Joe, who couldn't wait to tie the knot. The long-awaited day finally arrived and the couple were beaming with joy and looking forward to starting life together. Life was exciting for the married couple who started their honeymoon by taking a holiday cruise. They then embarked on touring the world in the first year of their marriage before they finally settled down. They planned to start having children a year into their marriage. Everything worked to plan and they had their first child a year later, bringing joy not just to their family but to those around them. Soon after, their second child came along. This worked well for the couple, who took on part-time jobs to accommodate childcare while balancing family life.

In the fifth year of their marriage, child number three came along, adding to the joy in the family. However, having three children brought not just joy but stretched the family resources further. The demand for time, money and school runs started to take a toll on the couple despite help and support from their immediate family. Joe started getting home late and this gradually went on to being unavailable for family time and being absent from childcare responsibilities. In addition, money was becoming scarce. Joe would also take frequent weekend breaks unannounced and not show up until several days later.

Friends' Stories

Karen noticed that something was amiss but was kept busy by their young children. She decided to hold everything together for the sake of maintaining stability for the family. She was struggling to get to work and to balance work with childcare. She shared these difficulties with friends and family, who advised her to talk to her husband in the first instance. But how could she do this when she hardly saw him? She finally managed to get hold of him on one of his rare drop-ins but they could not come to any resolution.

Joe continued to give excuses about having lots of work and saying that he needed to work hard and provide for the family. Worse was to come, however, when Karen started noticing Joe walking away from her when talking on the phone. On one occasion, Karen answered her husband's phone, only to hear another woman on the other end. She was later to learn that this was where the problem lay: Joe was actually seeing another woman! Everything now made sense. The frequent weekends away from home, the diminishing finances and odd behaviour all came down to this one thing: Joe was seeing someone else.

Karen was heartbroken. This was her childhood sweetheart and the father of her children. She still loved him but hated what he was now doing to her and their children. She was emotionally drained and was even struggling to work. Before she could get a handle on anything, her much loved husband packed his belongings and left the family home one morning in clear sight of the family. This was like a bad dream. The children were screaming and crying 'Daddy, don't leave us alone!'. All this fell on deaf ears as Joe quickly got into his car and drove off. This was the last they would hear from him. Meanwhile, Karen was broken in pieces and in total bewilderment as to what to do next.

With the help of family and friends, it would take the next five years for Karen to get back on her feet again. She said that trust was the one thing that would take a very long time to recover.

Sue's Story

Sue was a 45-year-old mother of two teenage sons. I had known Sue for several years, having met her at University while completing my postgraduate studies. Sue was known to be meticulous and highly organised in all that she did. She was a bubbly, outgoing woman whose joy filled everywhere she went. She loved her children and would always talk about them to friends and share the progress they made in school. When I met Sue at a school event which both our children attended, we were both excited to see each other and agreed to catch up for a chat.

It was a real joy to finally catch up at my house and we both looked forward to a great time of companionship. However, as soon as we sat down for a coffee, I saw a totally different woman. The bubbly woman was transformed into a shy and timid person who only spoke in limited words. She could hardly look at me and I struggled to come to terms with the woman who sat opposite me. She was literally looking over her shoulder and appeared to be in deep thought during our conversation. She had also lost a lot of weight and kept checking her phone for a call she seemed to be expecting. Breaking the ice was difficult, given the circumstances. I started the conversation by taking us back to our days at university. At this point, I saw a glimmer of a distant smile. As we recalled the good old days, Sue started to relax and we progressed to a deeper personal talk. But I was not prepared for what she was to say next.

Sue told me that she had recently separated from her husband of 15 years. Worse still, despite moving away from the family home, her ex-husband was still stalking her. Sue said she had gone through extreme physical and emotional abuse in the presence of her children. She had over the years tried to protect the family but could endure it no more.

José (Sue's husband) was a short, muscular and athletic man. He was loved by all who knew him and was known to be a very hard-working man. He loved his drink and was well known by other men in the local pub as a no no-sense person – but one who was very quick tempered. In one incident, he had head-locked one of the men and would not let go until he passed out. Such was José's reputation that no one dared to challenge him, not even about his relationship with Sue.

José had persistently abused Sue over the years by criticising her and even threatening to strangle her - literally on a daily basis. He would go out and come back in the early hours, demanding hot food among other things. Sue would stay awake until late and cook for him to ensure that he got a hot meal. She then had to sit and watch him eat. On many occasions, José would refuse food and would start arguments out of the blue that would culminate in him physically assaulting her or even throwing the food at her. Sue could not recount the number of times she had visited the local hospital and explained that she felt like she was walking on eggshells. She went on to tell me that, during one of these episodes, José came into the home late at night and threatened to kill the whole family! This was Sue's turning point. She had to make the decision to save her children and, at that point, she decided to leave him.

Sue moved to rented accommodation with her children, fully aware of the risks José posed. This was not far from the truth because, by the next day, José had made endless phone calls and left threatening messages on her phone. Sue was very scared and rang the police to deal with the situation. Unfortunately, this did not deter José. In one incident, Sue asked a local plumber to sort out a drainage problem at her new address. Unbeknown to her, José was just around the corner, waiting for the plumber to get back to his van. He instigated an argument and was ready to fight. The problem for him was that - in his opinion - the plumber should never have had any contact with his wife. The police had to be involved yet again. The plumber was not able to finish the work and she had to arrange for someone else to complete the job. Such was Sue's fear that she could not leave the house or socialise with friends.

Sue did however manage to get support for the children and protection against her ex-husband's abusive behaviour, including legal help to deter José from getting close to her new address. She told me that the issue of fear was something she was still working on with the help of counsellors but this would take a long while to resolve.

Biblical Examples of Single Mothers

Chapter 4

Hagar (Genesis 21)

The story of Hagar in the book of Genesis is heart-breaking. It is easy to label Hagar as the woman who was 'meddling' with Sarah's marriage until you understand her story in context. Hagar was a slave owned by Sarah, Abraham's wife, who had been infertile for a long time. In those days, it was considered that slaves could also be used by their master as concubines for the purpose of 'breeding' more slaves. Fortunately for Hagar, this was not the case but, instead, Sarah wanted to use Hagar as a surrogate mother.

Sarah told her husband that God had prevented her from having children. She then took Hagar and gave her to her husband to sleep with. It is clear in the Bible that this was not Hagar's plan and she probably never thought that she would have a child with her mistress's husband. One could argue that she was coerced into taking part in a union that she never planned for. She may have responded this way in part by being forced to be obedient to her mistress Sarah. No sooner had she conceived a baby, however, than all the trouble started. Hagar now looked down on her mistress and, in return, Sarah started to treat her harshly. As a result, the pregnant Hagar ran away to the desert.

We learn that, while in the desert, Hagar encountered God who instructed her to go back to Sarah and submit to her authority. She therefore went back to Sarah and started living with her again. In Genesis 21, Sarah by now - despite her age - had her own child, Isaac, and the boys grew up together. One day, however, Sarah spotted Ismael (Hagar's son) mocking her son Isaac. This annoyed her and she instructed Abraham to send both Hagar and her son away. Abraham was distressed by this but God instructed him to do as Sarah had told him.

Hagar and Ishmael were sent away the following morning and given just water and bread to survive on. When the water ran out, Hagar abandoned Ishmael under the bushes as 'she didn't want to see the boy die'. This was clearly a desperate scenario where a single mother had exhausted all options and left him to avoid seeing her son die of hunger. We are not told where she slept or lived. It's possible that she slept in the wilderness with the obvious risk to her life and that of her son. We again see God intervening in Hagar's life and that of her son and performing a miracle where He provides water. We know that this was a success story as the child survived and we now have many generations stemming from Ishmael's line.

Elijah and the Widow at Zarephath (1 Kings 17:10)

This is the story of a woman who was widowed and had an only son. God tells Elijah the prophet to go to Zarephath, a widow whom God had instructed to provide food for him. Then, as now, widows were largely seen as being disadvantaged and this widow was one in great need. Why would God instruct Elijah to go to a widow in order for her to provide food for other people? And one who was in need? Could this have been a situation where God wanted to show His love for those perceived to be lowly and disadvantaged?

There surely would have been plenty of other people that God could have used but He specifically chose to use a widow. He would miraculously bless this woman who chose to be obedient by serving God through Elijah.

The scriptures continue to explain that, when the prophet Elijah met her, she was gathering sticks to cook what she described as her last meal. The scriptures do not tell us how she was widowed. Nonetheless, the Bible clearly gives an account of a woman in desperate circumstances. The woman, who had an only son, didn't have enough to eat and told Elijah that she had less than a biscuit to survive on. The conversation between the widow and the prophet is thought provoking: 'I have a handful of flour in a jar and a little oil in a bottle; you found me scratching together just enough firewood to make my last meal for my son and me; after we eat, we'll die.' One can safely assume that there were a host of other unmet needs in the house. Is it possible that her rent was outstanding? What about water and other basic needs? There is an air of hopelessness in her response to Elijah: 'Eat our last meal and die'. The story graphically illustrates the struggle typical of a single mother with the added responsibilities of a dependent child.

As shown in the story of Hagar, God always had and still has a plan for those in hopeless situations. Psalm 68:5 says 'Father of the fatherless and protector of widows, is God in his holy habitation.' He who numbers the hairs on our heads will certainly not turn away from the children living as orphans.

We see the hand of God working in the widow's life when Elijah performed a miracle and her jar did not run out of meal and her bottle of oil didn't become empty. The woman who was preparing her last meal to eat and die now had plenty to eat and keep as stock! It is unbelievable what God can do by turning hopeless situations to hope and emptiness to abundance. Another success story!

The Widow's Oil (2 Kings 4:1-7)

This is a story about a woman who is not named but is referred to as the wife of a man from the guild of prophets. Her husband had died and left her in debt. The debt collectors were now coming to take her only two sons as slaves for the payment of the debt.

The woman, bereft at what was to happen to her sons, had reached out to the prophet Elisha and asked for help. Elisha asked the woman what she wanted him to do and went on to ask what she had in the house. To this, she replied 'Only a small jar of oil'. Elisha then asked her to send her sons to borrow empty containers

- and not just a few but all that they could find. God was about to perform a mighty miracle which would surprise the woman.

The story tells us that the woman and her sons followed the instruction of the prophet Elisha and filled up all their containers with oil from the little oil they had. The woman then sold some of the oil to pay off the debt and she had plenty left to support her and her two sons. This was extraordinary! The woman who was just a few minutes from having her sons taken away was now swimming in abundance.

This is another clear demonstration of how God met the need of a widow in a miraculous way.

The Persistent Widow (Luke 18:1-8)

The story of this widow in the book of Luke is distressing, to say the least. This story was presented as a parable by Jesus to his disciples and a clear demonstration of the great love and mercy that God has for us. The story emphasises the importance of persistence and the need to pray without ceasing.

The parable gives an account of a 'desperate' widow who was seeking justice and legal protection from her adversary. She faced a judge who 'did not fear God or respect any man'. What hope was there for this woman in the face of an arrogant person who nonetheless held a powerful office? If he didn't have any respect for a man, what recognition would he have for a woman, let alone a widow? Would the story of this widow have been different had her husband been alive? This was also a time when widows were viewed as desperate and needy people and this judge would have been very much aware of this. Who was, or where was, her support network? Did she have a family or neighbours who should have provided this support? Did she belong to a church or a community group? Is it possible that those close to her could potentially have been the cause of her pain?

However, the widow was persistent and kept going to the judge for justice. She had no other way to turn but she was determined not to let go and knew that this was the only way she would get justice. The judge, 'tired of being bothered because she was becoming an intolerable annoyance,' gave her justice and legal protection in order to get her out of the way.

Whilst the moral of the story is to persist in prayer to God who loves and answers us, one cannot fail to draw from the story the misery that surrounded this woman. She refused to be fobbed off and remained tenacious, knowing that this was where her answer lay.

One can draw parallels from the persistence of this woman to the experiences of many single parents. They are conscious of the fact that there is no one else to stand up for them and therefore fight with all their might.

My experience, and that of all these women, reflects the difficult experiences single women face. Single women continue to struggle on their own with few people or no-one to turn for help. The stigma attached to singlehood makes it difficult for them to actively seek help. This presents the church and the wider community with a great opportunity to fulfil the biblical mandate to care for widows and single parents. One thing that is positive in all these accounts is that God comes through in a powerful way every time.

The Impact of Single Parenting on the Parent

Chapter 5

THERE IS LITTLE INFORMATION about the hardships of the 'single father as a care-giver'. Single fathers are fewer in numbers but - in most cases - do an amazing job. Little is understood about the impact of singlehood on fathers, perhaps due to the relatively small numbers reported. On the other hand, there is a great deal written about the hardships of single mothers. Households of single mothers tend to find difficulty with the lack of help they receive. In most cases, single mothers find it difficult to find help because there is a lack of support, whether from the other parent or from other family members.

The accounts given above (both personal and biblical) paint a rather grim picture of the emotional impact experienced by single parents. The biblical examples highlight widows prepared to protect their children at any cost, strong women who went to great lengths to protect their children, good examples for every single mother.

In the majority of cases, single parents are not prepared for the breakdown in their relationships which often comes at a time of significant stress in looking after young children. For some of these parents, the busy schedule of housework etc means there is no time to take care of themselves. This was my experience. I failed to get time to go out for a coffee and, even when I had the time, I lacked the finances to do so.

My experience, and that of most single parents, demonstrates the overwhelming nature of a vulnerable situation, leaving a situation of hopelessness and helplessness. Without help, I was not far from depression and anxiety. Some single parents don't know where to start from, some lose their jobs, friends or even contact with family members. Most end up forming new relationships as a way of escaping from their pain and sorrow. However, some of these new relationships can be detrimental to them and their children. Others indulge in substances (e.g. drugs or alcohol) as a coping mechanism.

There are however some who choose to bring up children on their own, despite the difficulties in doing so. I decided to make that choice, but I know that those who do so are far and few and have to brave themselves to taking up both the roles of a father and mother. I literally gave up my life and put all my energy into my children.

There is clearly no right or wrong way to do single parenting. Single parents have to make decisions at various points in their journey. Having support from friends and family during this difficult time helps form stability and balanced decision making. However, those parents who have managed to go through the process alone have said that it was worth going through; despite being the most difficult time in their lives, it was also the most rewarding.

Many parents have emerged stronger and more resilient and a source of pride to their children who, having succeeded in life, make positive reference to their mothers who brought them up single-handedly.

The Impact of Single Parenting on Children

Chapter 6

MY CHILDREN STRUGGLED with the notion of absent father. This was perhaps because I was in a similar place to them and, for a long time, feeling sorry for myself. They became angry and, at times, fearful. However, I regularly spoke to them and reminded them that they had a special Father in heaven.

At one point in our lives, a youth teacher and a close family friend took it upon himself to mentor my sons. This was a miracle for me. All this time I had been praying for a male role model and here was a young man willing to be that person to the boys!

This was a real turn-around and they built a special relationship where they could discuss openly what was troubling them. I will be forever grateful to this young friend. However, this is probably the exception rather than the rule, as the following examples illustrate.

Alex

Alex and his two siblings grew up in a single parent home. Their father used to travel a lot and was hardly ever at home. Alex always struggled to understand why their home was different. Mum would do all she could to engage him in activities appropriate to his age. She would take him to football club, karate and swimming, just to name a few. Alex would watch other children being picked up by their fathers and he would burst into tears. He never told his mother why he would cry when she went to pick him up. Around the age of 8, Alex would express his feelings by drawing pictures of his father, asking when he would be coming back home. This was his way of communicating his pain to his mother.

As it turned out, Alex's mum was equally in a vulnerable state and was unable to address this with her son as she too was hurting. She took him to a nearby club where he was able to find mentors who worked with him over the years. He managed to do well in school and go to university. Now in a high-flying career, Alex recounts how he found it difficult to comprehend his young life. He has now devoted his life to supporting those in similar situations.

Ben

Ben's father walked out on his family when Ben was hardly three years old and Ben's sister Sally was only a year old. On this fateful day, Ben's father informed the family that he was briefly going to the shop to pick up a newspaper. That was the last time Ben saw his father. The first few years were the most difficult for Ben and the family. Mum didn't have a stable job and was unable to work as Sally was still very young. By the age of four, Ben had learnt how to prepare Sally's toilet bag and supervise Sally when mum went out to the shops, which was risky as well as being illegal.

Life went from bad to worse and the two children had to be left in the care of a neighbour while mum went to work. It didn't take long for Ben to start exhibiting behavioural problems. By the age of 7, he had started going onto the streets with local boys and was committing petty crimes. At age 10, Ben had been introduced to smoking 'pot' and was hardly ever going to school. Ben's mother found it exceedingly difficult to manage the home as well as work. By the time Ben entered his teenage years, he was already in a young offenders' institution for grievously assaulting another person. Meanwhile Sally had started rebelling against her mother, who was by now in despair.

These examples illustrate that, although a single parent with adequate resources and support is able to provide a stable, nurturing home in which children thrive just as well as those who have two parents, children can become vulnerable and at risk of poor outcomes in situations where a single parent is struggling with resources, and has little time, energy or skill for parental duties.

Children are always negatively impacted by any family breakdown, and more so where there is no support. Children are left to deal with the uncertainty of a 'broken home' while their emotions are still too immature to cope with the finite details. For some children, this translates into negative feelings of blaming themselves for the breakdown and wishing they could do something to change the situation. For others the situation is terrifying enough and, with nowhere else to go, they exhibit behaviours of being fearful or aggressive. Fearful because they don't know what the future will look like or who will be supporting them, and fearful of the likelihood that they will be the subject of talk in school, and possibly bullying.

The few who show signs of aggression often do so as a way of fighting feelings of fear. Being aggressive is their way of sending a message to others that they are strong and able to cope with what has been thrown at them. They want to be seen as being able to handle the situation whilst inwardly they are struggling. Support for children during these times is crucial and this is where family and close friends and, indeed, the community must come in and provide that shoulder to cry on.

The child growing up in a single parent home is (more often than not) given extra responsibilities due to the absence of the other parent. They are likely to be left on their own or to look after their younger siblings whilst the custodial parent goes to work or to shop. Regular household chores will most certainly be an expectation, not a choice. In homes where the father is absent, boys especially can be expected to take on the role of 'the man of the house' at a very young age.

A close friend, who is also a single mother, reported that her son had assumed the father's role at the age of 12! He would be taking responsibility for his younger siblings in a way similar to an adult: a really big and inappropriate task at this tender age. Whilst all children should be taught coping strategies for when they grow up, the difference for a child living in a single parent home is that nothing prepares them for the steep learning curve they face. They can find themselves in a situation where they have to grow up very quickly whilst still coming to terms with the loss of one parent.

For some, 'being a child' is no longer possible as the resident parent can sometimes become dependent on them. For example, a parent may want to share their experiences of the other parent with the child. This puts the child in a difficult situation as the other parent is, as far as they are concerned, an 'equal' parent to them and, in some situations, the child could still be in contact with the other parent. This co-dependency between the child and the parent can continue into adulthood, potentially making it difficult for the young person to start a life of their own.

The majority of single parents have to juggle work to make ends meet. In order to do this, and without available childcare facilities, most leave their children in the care of friends and family. In most cases, this works well and the single parent is able to work around family and friends. In a smaller number of cases, though, leaving children with others increases the risk of them being abused by family, friends or neighbours. Where this is the case, the child grows up with a view that the world is unjust and unkind.

A recent high-profile case of abuse reported that the alleged perpetrator himself experienced abusive behaviour from the age of 9 while in the care of an older sibling. Having been brought up by a single mother, he would be left in the care of his older sister while his mother went to work. No sooner would the mother leave the house than the older sister would abuse him and his other sibling. The behaviour he learnt at this tender age continued into adulthood when he began abusing others. Whilst all abuse is totally unacceptable, it is clear that the circumstances the young person was brought up in contributed to the abusive man he became.

There are however plenty of situations where this is not the case and a child growing up in a single parent family gets support from family and friends. Where such support is available, the outcomes for these children are no worse than if they had had both parents living with them, and there are plenty of examples where this is the case.

Single Parenting and Society

Chapter 7

'IT TAKES A VILLAGE to raise a child' is an African proverb that means that an entire community of people must interact with a child for the child to experience and grow in a safe and healthy environment. The responsibility of the society to contribute to raising the child should never be underestimated. The initial step is the recognition that single parenting is a difficult task. Provision of facilities and support is crucial to ensure support is available for both the parents and the children. Where single parents are unable to sustain themselves and their children, the cost to the government is significant.

Whilst most single parents do an amazing job on their own, there remains a stigma that surrounds them. A significant number of people in our society have portrayed single mothers as needy, desperate and incapable of holding a family together. Sadly, these views extend further afield, including to some churches which should be at the forefront, fighting for these families. As long as this view remains, single parents will have no voice and will have to fight a much tougher battle to be able to stand on their own. It becomes difficult for single parents to receive support when this view is still held by society.

Churches, and the community at large, have a great opportunity to address the needs of these women. A few churches have taken steps to engage with single parents and their children, for example instituting single parent programmes which are playing a key role in supporting families with positive outcomes.

Things I Have Learnt as a Single Parent

Chapter 8

THIS CHAPTER SETS out six things I have learned during fifteen years of being a single parent:

1. Stay positive

This is easier to say than do, especially when everything happening around is depressing, the option to remain is negative and therefore depression seems justified. However, accepting this state of affairs would only make things worse. I experienced this first-hand and came to the conclusion that entertaining negative thoughts would only attract people with similar views and negatively impact my health and wellbeing. I had to make the decision to deliberately look for the good in a bad situation. I learnt how to speak positively in the midst of doom and gloom. I would speak to myself and make statements like, 'It's going to be fine;' 'I can do all things through Christ who gives me the strength' and 'I'm wonderfully and fearfully made'. In due course, the power of the spoken word became a reality. I started seeing positive changes in myself and my children. I finally had a reason to wake up and get outside and smile at other people. I had not realised how much of a sad person I had become. Now that things were starting to change, I had every reason to keep speaking positively. I deliberately looked out for things to be grateful for. This started to work for me and for my children.

2. You are not guilty

One of the challenges I faced was that of guilt consciousness. I felt that things would have been better if I had done more to save my marriage. I blamed myself for how I had handled previous conversations. The situation was exacerbated by a cultural perception that, if a marriage was failing, then the woman was to blame. My mind was a battlefield where I fought with myself over what I could have done to improve the situation. I had grown up as a timid person and going through this difficult patch of my life initially added to my timidity.

Ironically, during this time, I worked as a domestic abuse adviser and would listen to survivors' stories of abuse. On a daily basis, I would encourage survivors and tell them things would change for the better. There were three key statements we gave as specialists in the field to all survivors: 'I believe you;' 'It's not your fault,' and 'There's help for you'. I had memorised these words and would speak them out loud without a thought. But I had never thought that that was exactly what I needed to hear for my own situation. Then I took some time to reflect on the very words I had used for these survivors and started speaking them to myself.

It worked! The power of words was evident. I didn't need to blame myself for my husband's choice to walk away from the family. I was not responsible for his decisions and I was free to make my own decisions.

3. Take care of yourself

Taking care of oneself has a direct impact on how we feel. Have you ever seen a smartly dressed person who knew they looked smart? The confidence in them is obvious; the smile and the body language speak for themselves.

Whilst important, it's the one area I had neglected over the years without realising it. My focus was on my children - full stop. I had failed to see how I could go and buy myself anything of value. Any money I saved was directed towards the children. In the absence of their father, I felt that I had the responsibility to fill the void. I would not let them miss anything and I worked extra hard to make it happen, albeit with much difficulty.

Had it not been for a dear sister, I would probably have worn myself out. She was open and honest and told me that I had to look after myself. She reminded me that it was OK to spend money on my hair, among other things. This was very liberating. Slowly I started taking better care of myself. I budgeted for my hair on a monthly basis and it felt great to visit my hairdresser and be pampered.

I also started to re-connect with friends, some of whom were going through a similar situation to myself. All along I'd thought I was the only one going through a difficult time. I was able to share my story with them and this was the beginning of my healing process.

4. Accept help

When going through a difficult patch in life, it's easy to think that people don't have time to help or that there's no need to bother them or that they don't care. In my case, this was the case, including a strong feeling of shame and being judged. I wanted to belong and have a sense of belonging; after all that's why I had got married. I became very sensitive to the false perception of single parents by others. In my world, everybody judged a single parent as a loser, failure and home breaker and didn't have time for them.

As such, it was difficult to see the help that was there, as I had built a solid wall around myself. The reality is that I was hurting from deep within and this repelled anyone who was sympathetic and willing to reach out. I have to add that there were people desiring to help but I was not in a place to receive it. Sadly for me, this only prolonged my years of pain. On reflection, I should have jumped at any and every bit of help available.

It took a prayerful friend to speak a work of knowledge to me. That's what got my attention. God is full of humour, He knew what I needed and it came at the right time. We were in a mid-week service and as soon as I stepped on stage to sing, this woman screamed in terror and was praying fervently! What a shock! However, I was to learn later that she had been praying for me and my family. Up until that time, I had not shared anything with her but she was able to narrate everything to me and tell me what God wanted me to do, part of which was to accept help. How extraordinary! I will never forget this woman who was so persistent and never gave up on me - she was certainly God sent. She prayed for me and with me. She made time and I'm sure she put up with a lot from me. I will forever be grateful to her and pray for abundant grace upon her life.

Unfortunately, this is not always the case for everyone and my advice is to always accept help from trusted people who are willing to help. There are genuine, kind people out there who want to help, so find space to allow this help to come through.

5. Trust in God

For some of us, faith is that one thing we hold on to when things go 'pear shaped'. For me, faith in God was the most important thing that saw me carry on from days to months to years. There were songs I sang over my situation, sermons I held on to. And I wrote most of my own songs during this time.

One of the best things I did was to learn to pray. This is where I developed an intimate relationship with God. I set up a private prayer space just for me and God. This was the space where I would cry my eyes out, then pray until I couldn't pray any further. I cannot tell you the dreams and encounters I received during this time. I believe these will all come to pass in my time. If there's one thing I'm grateful for during this time, it's my relationship with God. He remains everything to me; a special friend, a confidant, a father; words cannot describe Him but all I needed and still need in my life is what I found in Him. I remain at peace with my children in His hands. He is absolutely able to do what He says in His word. After all, I'm the clay and He's the potter.

This intimacy still remains and I could not trade it for anything. I can even sense His presence as I write. If He did it for me, surely, He can do it for anyone.

6. Being a steward

As parents, we are only stewards of our children. Children are God's creation and if anyone cares more about them than us, it's the Creator Himself. My greatest fear was about my children and how they would cope with all that was happening to them. I had many questions about what would become of them. I grew up in a family where my father was always at home. As children, we knew the time he would leave for work and get back home. As such I had never imagined being in a home without both parents.

This was therefore a new world for me. I cried daily for my children: why did this have to happen to them? I felt they didn't deserve it and they never would understand. I watched them ask questions, most of which I didn't have answers for, or I felt they were too young to understand the truth. I feared they would become rebels. My fears certainly had some impact on them as I could start seeing my anxiety in them. If things had to change, it had to start with me.

My friend was on my case again. She reminded me that children are safe in God's hands. You're only a steward, she would remind me. There was no need to worry myself. God had them and He would be a father to them with or without their father. I learnt to leave them in God's hands through prayer. Gradually I was at peace that they were in better hands than my constant worry. I also became aware that, as things started to change for me, the children picked it up and I could see self-confidence returning to all of us.

Final Thoughts

Chapter 9

As I said at the beginning, single parenting for some people is a choice which should be respected. There are also those who have chosen to remain single after finding themselves in difficult situations, for example those whose partners are deceased or whose partners have left them. Irrespective of the situation you may find yourself in, the aim is to get the best out of the situation for your sake and that of your children.

For me, being single was never a choice. I was very idealistic and this experience hit me hard. I have learnt a lot though: I am no longer the idealist person I used to be and much more realistic and practical. Although it's been difficult, I would not trade the experiences for anything. In writing this book, I spoke to a lot of single parents who reported that they learnt more about themselves, their friends and about their faith through their experiences. Some drew much closer to God during these difficult moments. Going through a difficult time taught them who their genuine friends were. Some took time to look after themselves in a way they had not done before - perhaps due to the fact that they appreciated life a lot more. They were able to develop close relationship with friends and those of faith developed complete dependence on God.

In situations where children were supported by family or friends, there was always a positive outcome. My children were beneficiaries of support from friends and are now reaping the benefits of a support system that every single parent desire to have. Studies have shown that children growing up in a single parent household, who are well supported by family and friends, enjoy positive childhood experiences with outcomes no worse from a child from a two-parent home.

There is the added benefit of extra skills single parents gain by being confident and self-reliant due to the need to manage two roles in the household and with no one to consult. There is also the opportunity to spend a lot more time with the child where possible, making the relationship between parent and child closer.

The biggest thing I took away from my experience is that challenges in life almost always happen for a reason. I have found that, depending on how we embrace these challenges, we come out much stronger and better. We must never forget the most important person in all this - ourselves. We can only look after others including our children when we have taken good care of ourselves. The ability to accept help in those difficult situations is a strength in itself. I found out that there are plenty of people willing to help and one needs to discern who these people are. In addition, I found out that giving of ourselves builds in us resilience and shifts our focus from self. It's when I started seeking

Final Thoughts

out those who were less fortunate than myself and needed help, that I realised how fortunate I was, despite living through what I perceived as my worst nightmare. Could the reason we sometimes feel helpless be the fact that we haven't lent a hand to those who are in greater need than ourselves? As I conclude, my very last piece of advice for those single parents struggling is that you are never alone and help is only an arm's length away.

References

Collins Dictionary Online: https://www.collinsdictionary.com/

Divorce rate for heterosexual couples hits 45-year low, figures show: The Independent, 26 September 2018

Hughes, Selwyn: Marriage as God Intended (2005)

The Single Mother Guide: https://singlemotherguide.com/

The Bible: New International Version

The Office for National Statistics - Single parents: https://www.ons.gov.uk/

Voltaire (1694-1778), writer and philosopher

Books by Lucie Muchina

Domestic Abuse: What every woman needs to know: A practical guide to domestic abuse in Church (2013)

Dare to Dream (2019)

www.ingramcontent.com/pod-product-compliance
Lightning Source LLC
Chambersburg PA
CBHW050447010526
44118CB00013B/1727